MARS OR BUST!

ORION AND THE MISSION TO DEEP SPACE

AILYNN COLLINS

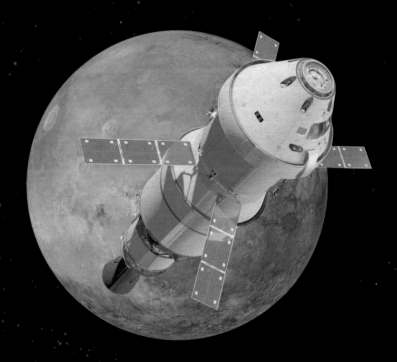

CONTENT CONSULTANT
SARAH RUIZ
Aerospace Engineer

CAPSTONE PRESS
a capstone imprint

Edge Books are published by Capstone Press,
1710 Roe Crest Drive, North Mankato, Minnesota 56003
www.capstonepub.com

Library of Congress Cataloging-in-Publication Data
Names: Collins, Ailynn, 1964– author.
Title: Mars or bust : Orion and the mission to deep space / by Ailynn Collins.
Description: North Mankato, Minnesota : Capstone Press, [2019] | Series: Edge books.
Future space | "Edge Books is published by Capstone Press." | Audience: Ages 8–9. |
Audience: Grades 4 to 6. Identifiers: LCCN 2019004841| ISBN 9781543572681 (hardcover) |
ISBN 9781543575149 (pbk.) | ISBN 9781543572766 (ebook pdf) Subjects: LCSH: Orion
spacecraft—Juvenile literature. | Space flight to Mars—Juvenile literature. | Manned space
flight—Juvenile literature. | Space vehicles—United States—Juvenile literature. | Mars
(Planet)—Exploration—Juvenile literature. Classification: LCC TL789.8.U6 O7535 2019 |
DDC 629.45/53—dc23 LC record available at https://lccn.loc.gov/2019004841

Editorial Credits
Michelle Parkin, editor; Laura Mitchell, designer; Jo Miller, media researcher;
Katy LaVigne, production specialist

Image Credits
NASA, Cover (Orion), 5, 10, 15, 19, 21; NASA/JPL – Caltech, 25, 27; NASA: Robert Markowitz, 12;
NASA: Roscosmos, 7; Newscom: MEGA/EM, 22, Photoshot/NASA/Atlas Photo Archive, 16, UPI/Joe
Marino – Bill Cantrell, 9, ZUMA Press/Lockheed Martin, 17; Science Source: Stocktrek Images/Frieso
Hoevelkamp, 28; Shutterstock: Nerthuz, Cover (Mars)

Design Elements
Capstone; Shutterstock: Audrius Birbilas

All internet sites appearing in back matter were available and accurate when this book was
sent to press.

Printed and bound in the United States of America.
PA70

TABLE OF CONTENTS

CHAPTER ONE

HOW FAR WE'VE COME

Fifty years ago, the first human stepped onto the moon. From 1969 until 1972, 11 more astronauts walked on the moon. Space agencies from around the world began building the **International Space Station** (ISS) in 1998. Since 2000, astronauts from 18 different countries have lived on the ISS while in space.

But scientists aren't stopping there. They want to go where people have never traveled before—into deep space. What will it take for humans to study **asteroids** and explore faraway worlds? Scientists and **engineers** have continued to create new technology to explore farther into space. They are making plans and building spacecraft. Someday soon we may see astronauts stepping onto Mars for the first time. Deep-space travel is moving closer to reality.

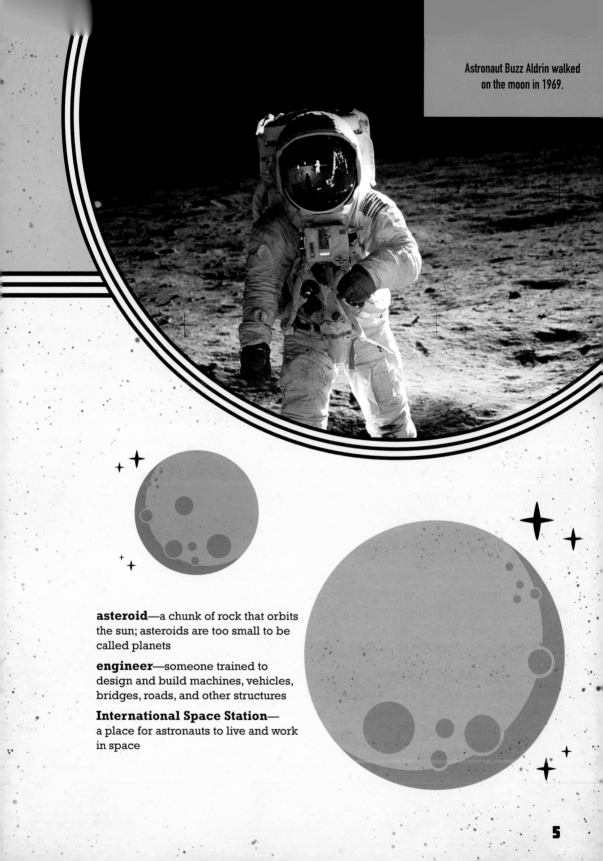

Astronaut Buzz Aldrin walked on the moon in 1969.

asteroid—a chunk of rock that orbits the sun; asteroids are too small to be called planets

engineer—someone trained to design and build machines, vehicles, bridges, roads, and other structures

International Space Station—a place for astronauts to live and work in space

DEEP SPACE:
THE NEXT FRONTIER

The ISS **orbits** more than 200 miles (322 kilometers) above Earth. This distance is considered Low Earth Orbit (LEO). LEO is between 99 and 1,200 miles (159 and 1,931 km) above Earth's surface. Many space missions have been within this distance.

Deep space goes beyond LEO. Sometimes called outer space, deep space is outside the pull of Earth's **gravity**. Deep space includes the moon and planets in our **solar system**. Scientists are designing more space missions to go farther than we've gone before.

orbit—to travel around an object in space

gravity—a force that pulls objects together; gravity pulls objects down toward the center of Earth

solar system—the sun and all the planets, moons, comets, and smaller bodies orbiting it

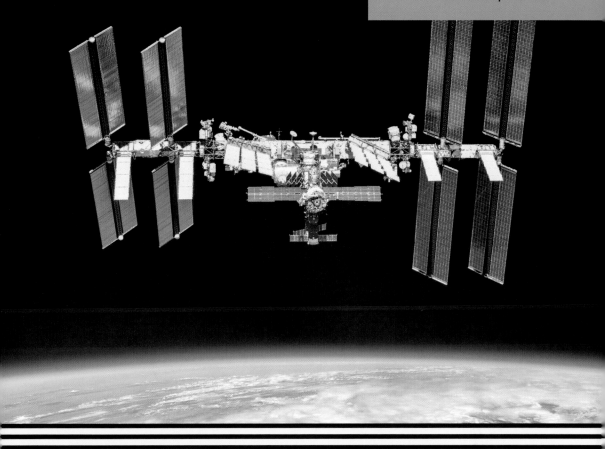

Gravity

Throw a ball up in the air. No matter how hard you throw it, the ball will always fall to the ground. This happens because of gravity. Gravity pulls objects toward the center of Earth. It keeps objects—and humans—from floating away into space.

To get a spacecraft into outer space, it has to escape Earth's gravity. To do that, it needs a large and powerful rocket.

CHAPTER TWO

ORION AND THE SLS

NASA, along with more than 1,000 **aerospace**, technology, and engineering companies, is building a rocket system to get spacecraft into deep space. The Space Launch System (SLS) will be the most advanced rocket system ever built. It's made to go farther into space than any rocket has gone before. The SLS is scheduled to launch in 2020. Scientists believe the SLS is the answer to getting humans into deep space.

But the SLS is only part of the solution. To explore new worlds in space, astronauts need a spacecraft. NASA and the European Space Agency (ESA) have built a spacecraft for the job. It's called the Orion Multi-Purpose Crew Vehicle.

SPACE FACT:

NASA stands for the National Aeronautics and Space Administration.

Before any spacecraft can carry astronauts into space, it must be tested first. Orion's first test was in 2014. NASA sent Orion into Earth's orbit without astronauts on board. It was launched on a Delta IV rocket. Orion traveled at a speed of 20,000 miles (32,187 km) per hour. Then it safely returned to Earth. The test flight was a success.

aerospace—the science and technology of jet flight and space travel

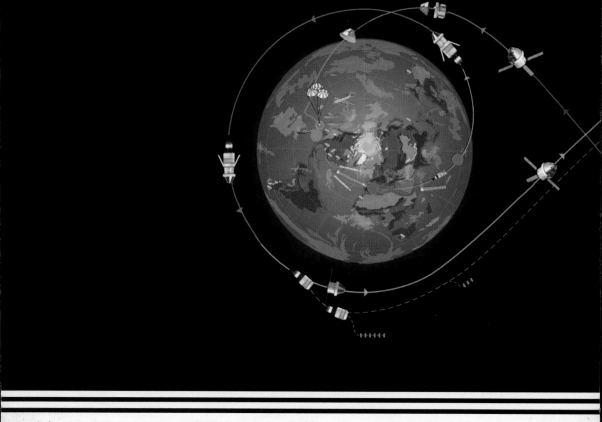

In 2020 scientists plan to test Orion again.
This mission is called Exploration Mission-1
(EM-1). Orion will sit on top of the SLS, 321 feet
(98 meters) above the launch pad. That's higher
than the Statue of Liberty! Together, Orion and
SLS will weigh more than 5 million pounds
(2.3 million kilograms). The SLS will push Orion
away from Earth at a speed up to 24,500 miles
(39,429 km) per hour.

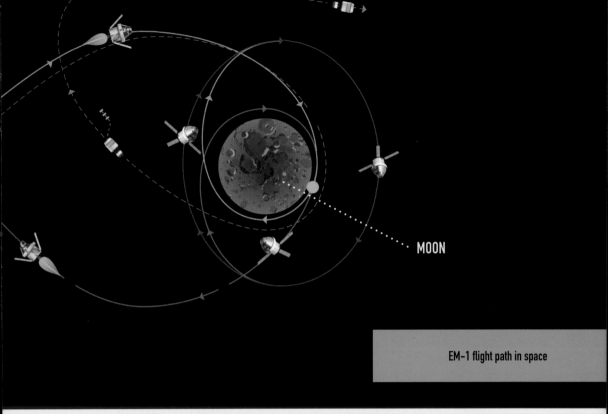

MOON

Once in space, Orion will separate from the SLS. Then it will travel 1.3 million miles (2.1 million km) around the moon and back to Earth. No astronauts will be on board this mission. Scientists need to make sure the rocket and spacecraft work as planned before adding astronauts.

part of the Orion spacecraft

SPACE FACT:

Orion's journey around
the moon will take
between eight days
and three weeks.

If Orion's EM-1 is a success, Orion's next mission will travel the same path. Exploration Mission-2 (EM-2) is scheduled for 2023. This time four astronauts will be on board. If the mission is successful, scientists hope Orion will take astronauts to Mars or even farther into space.

People Behind the Astronauts

Astronauts are an important part of any successful space mission. But hundreds of people work on the ground providing support to the astronauts. These workers include scientists, engineers, technicians, designers, pilots, and radio operators. Some gather data from spacecraft and launch facilities. Others analyze data and make decisions based on their findings.

If problems arise in space, there's little time to make critical decisions. This is why engineers and scientists do **simulations** with astronauts. They work together to find solutions to issues. That way, they can be ready if the same issues happen in space.

simulation—the act of imitating what will or could happen in real life

CHAPTER THREE

LIVING IN SPACE

What will astronauts need to survive in deep space? Humans need air, food, and water to live. Astronauts also need space to move, especially during long missions. And the spacecraft will need to be kept at the correct temperature.

When designing Orion, NASA and ESA kept all of this in mind. Astronauts will be seated in the Orion crew **module** during liftoff. This area will also be a living space during their mission.

module—a separate section that can be linked to other parts

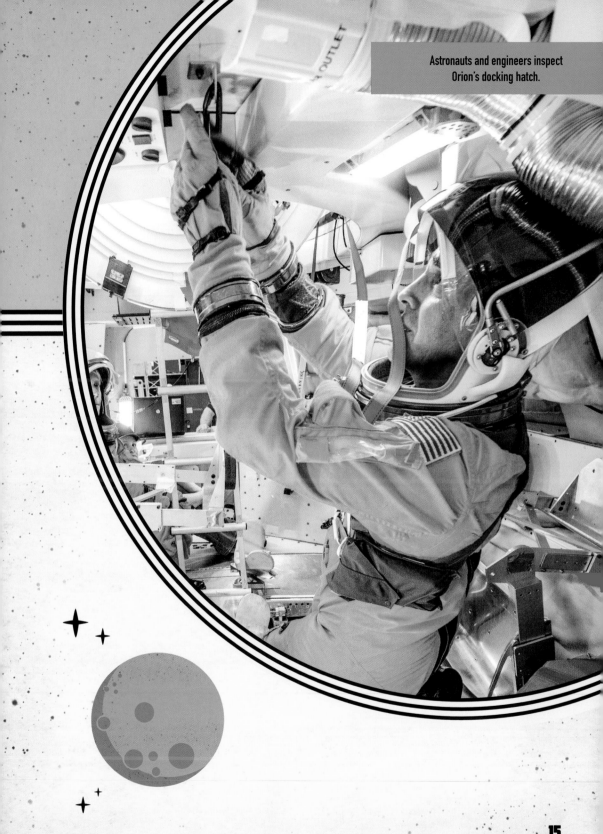

Astronauts and engineers inspect Orion's docking hatch.

Orion's crew module can fit up to six astronauts on board. It will be about 16 feet (5 m) wide and 10 feet (3 m) high. No matter how hot or cold space is outside, the module will stay at 72 degrees Fahrenheit (22 degrees Celsius). Astronauts won't have a lot of room, but scientists will try to make them as comfortable as possible.

a 2015 digital drawing of Orion

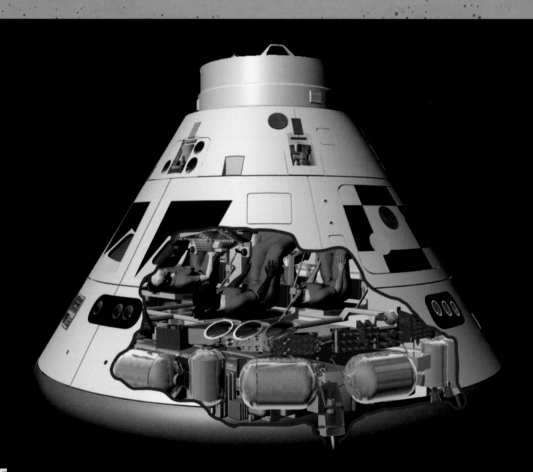

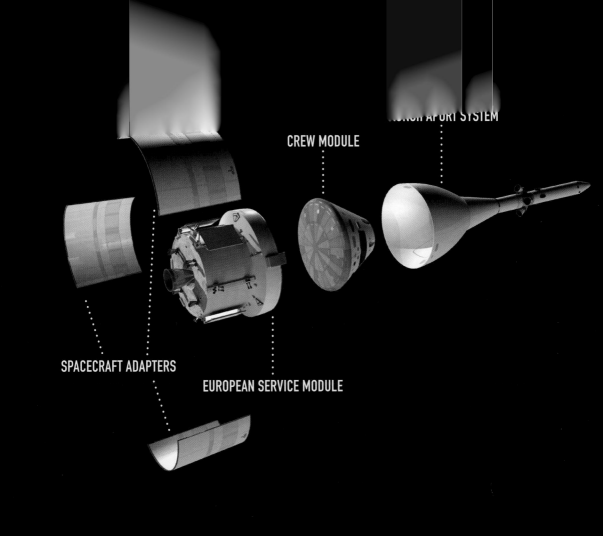

CREW MODULE

LAUNCH ABORT SYSTEM

SPACECRAFT ADAPTERS

EUROPEAN SERVICE MODULE

a view of what the inside of Orion's crew module will look like

As space missions last longer, astronauts
will need more room to move inside. Scientists will
base new designs on how astronauts live on the ISS.

ESA built the service module for Orion. This part provides the spacecraft's water, air, and electricity. The service module also holds tanks of fuel for Orion's engines. The module will have **solar panels**. The panels will gather energy from the sun to provide electricity for the spacecraft. Three panels make up a solar array wing. Each wing is 22 feet (6.7 m) long. The spacecraft has four solar array wings. When Orion is in darkness, rechargeable batteries will store power until the solar panels can be used again.

At the end of Orion's mission, the service module will fall away. Only the crew module carrying the astronauts will return to Earth. Any high-speed object traveling through the **atmosphere** must withstand temperatures as high as 5,000 degrees F (2,760 degrees C). To keep astronauts safe as Orion speeds back toward Earth, scientists created a heat shield. It's the largest heat shield in the world and is located at the base of the crew module. The shield will focus the heat away from the astronauts inside. Once Orion gets through the atmosphere, strong parachutes will help it land safely in the ocean. Then U.S. Navy ships will pick up the astronauts.

solar panel—a flat surface that collects sunlight and turns it into power
atmosphere—the layer of gases that surrounds some planets, dwarf planets, and moons

Solar panels will collect the sun's energy to make electricity for Orion.

CHAPTER FOUR

NEXT STOP, MARS

One of NASA's space exploration plans is called Moon to Mars. The moon is much closer to Earth than Mars. This makes it an ideal place to develop new technology and systems for deep space. What we build and learn on the moon can be used on future missions to Mars.

Many countries are planning missions to the moon. China and ESA hope to build a habitat there called a moon village. This permanent village is seen as the first step to reaching and exploring Mars. China and ESA hope to build the village by 2030. India also plans to send astronauts to the moon. Several space agencies, including NASA and ESA, are working together on a lunar space station called the Lunar Orbital Platform-Gateway.

The Lunar Orbital Platform-Gateway will
be the first crewed space station near the moon.
Scientists want it to include a small habitat for
the crew, communications station, science lab,
and docking station for visiting spacecraft. The
Gateway would test long-term missions in
deep-space environments.

One day the Aurora Station will be able to hold six guests in space.

Aurora Station

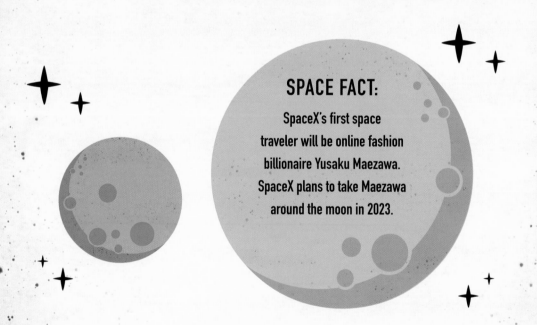

SPACE FACT:

SpaceX's first space traveler will be online fashion billionaire Yusaku Maezawa. SpaceX plans to take Maezawa around the moon in 2023.

SPACE TOURISM

Imagine if you could go to the moon for summer vacation or take a ride around Earth in a spacecraft. This may be possible sooner than you think. Private companies such as SpaceX, Virgin Galactic, and Blue Origin are planning such missions. Tickets will cost between $200,000 and $300,000. The first flights will be to suborbital space, about 62 miles (100 km) above Earth. But someday people could take one- to two-week vacations on space stations orbiting Earth!

CHAPTER FIVE

THE RED PLANET

NASA's Moon to Mars Exploration mission is just one of many exploration plans. Private companies and countries such as China are also interested in sending humans to Mars.

Right now unmanned **probes** are located on Mars. Scientists use them to study different parts of the planet. Scientists are also learning about the atmosphere, land, and climate of Mars. The latest probe to land on the red planet was NASA's InSight. It landed near Mars's equator on November 26, 2018. InSight's mission will last at least two years.

probe—a small, unmanned spacecraft sent to gather data

InSight took a photo
of itself in December 2018.

Two tiny **satellites** followed InSight to its destination on Mars. Known as Mars Cube One (MarCO), these satellites served as a relay system for InSight to communicate with Earth during its landing.

Farther Than We Imagined

In 1977 NASA launched two probes into space. Voyager 1 and Voyager 2 took photos of Jupiter, Saturn, Uranus, and Neptune. When their mission was over, the probes kept going deeper into space. They continue to collect data today.

The Voyager probes have gone farther than any human-made object has ever traveled. In 2012 Voyager 1 crossed into **interstellar** space. This part of space is beyond the sun's magnetic field. Voyager 2 followed in November 2018. The Voyager probes will continue traveling through space until their power runs out.

The MarCO satellites are a type of CubeSat.
CubeSats are small, boxy satellites are about the size
of a briefcase. MarCO became the first CubeSats to
go beyond Earth's orbit into deep space. They flew
within 2,500 miles (4,023 km) of Mars's surface.

interstellar—between the stars, most often used to describe travel from
one star to another

PROBES AND RADIATION

Sending probes to Mars helps scientists learn about potential dangers to humans, including space **radiation**. The atmosphere and a magnetic field help shield Earth from the sun's radiation. There's also radiation in space. Mars doesn't have the same protection.

Today's spacecraft are built to protect astronauts from this radiation. But living on a planet without an Earth-like atmosphere could expose people to high levels of radiation. Data collected from probes could help scientists build better habitats for humans on new planets.

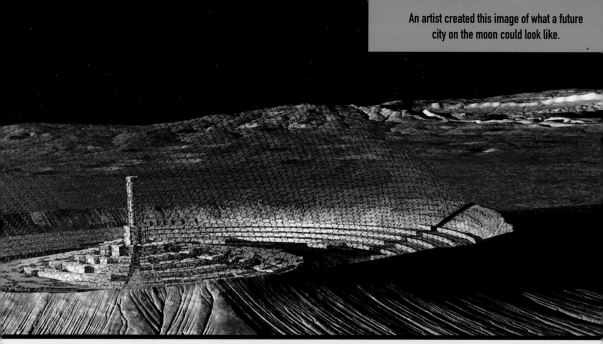

Many exciting developments in space exploration are happening all over the world. As technology advances, so do the opportunities to explore deep space. Perhaps one day, scientists will create rockets and spacecraft to take us to distant planets. We may even see people living on the moon or vacationing on Mars in the near future!

radiation—rays of energy given off by certain elements

GLOSSARY

aerospace (AIR-oh-spayss)—the science and technology of jet flight and space travel

asteroid (AS-tuh-royd)—a chunk of rock that orbits the sun; asteroids are too small to be called planets

atmosphere (AT-muh-sfeer)—the layer of gases that surrounds some planets, dwarf planets, and moons

engineer (en-juh-NEER)—someone trained to design and build machines, vehicles, bridges, roads, and other structures

gravity (GRAV-uh-tee)—a force that pulls objects together; gravity pulls objects down toward the center of Earth

International Space Station (in-tur-NASH-uh-nuhl SPAYSS STAY-shuhn)—a place for astronauts to live and work in space

interstellar (in-tur-STEL-lahr)—between the stars, most often used to describe travel from one star to another

module (MOJ-ool)—a separate section that can be linked to other parts

orbit (OR-bit)—to travel around an object in space

probe (PROHB)—a small, unmanned spacecraft sent to gather data

radiation (ray-dee-AY-shun)—rays of energy given off by certain elements

simulation (sim-yuh-LAY-shuhn)—the act of imitating what will or could happen in real life

solar panel (SOH-lur PAN-uhl)—a flat surface that collects sunlight and turns it into power

solar system (SOH-lur SISS-tuhm)—the sun and all the planets, moons, comets, and smaller bodies orbiting it

READ MORE

Jenkins, Martin. *Exploring Space: From Galileo to the Mars Rover and Beyond.* Somerville: MA: Candlewick Press, 2017.

Silverman, Buffy. *Mars Missions: A Space Discovery Guide. Space Discovery Guides.* Minneapolis: Lerner Publications, 2017.

Spilsbury, Richard, and Louise Spilsbury. *Fly to Mars!: Forces in Space. Feel the Force.* Chicago: Heinemann Raintree, 2016.

INTERNET SITES

NASA Mars Exploration
https://mars.nasa.gov/participate/funzone/

National Geographic Kids Mission to Mars
https://kids.nationalgeographic.com/explore/space/mission-to-mars/#mars-planet.jpg

INDEX